PICTURE LIBRARY

MOUNTAINS

PICTURE LIBRARY
MOUNTAINS

Norman Barrett

Franklin Watts

London   New York   Sydney   Toronto

© 1989 Franklin Watts

First published in the USA by
Franklin Watts Inc
387 Park Avenue South
New York
NY 10016

US ISBN: 0-531-10
Library of Congress Catalog Card
Number 8 –

Printed in Italy

Designed by
Barrett and Weintroub

Photographs by
Arizona Office of Tourism
Australian Overseas Information
    Service, London
N.S. Barrett
Crater Lake Natural History
    Association (artist Paul Rockwood)
French Government Tourist Office
GeoScience Features
Nick Howarth
Remote Source
South American Pictures
Sólarfilma
Survival Anglia
Tourism Canada
Travel Montana
Xinhua News Agency

Illustration by
Rhoda and Robert Burns

Technical Consultant
Keith Lye

Contents

Introduction

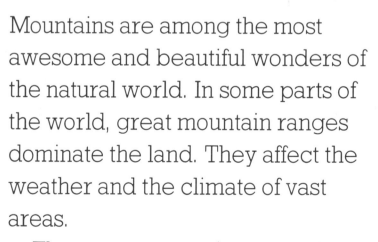

Mountains are among the most awesome and beautiful wonders of the natural world. In some parts of the world, great mountain ranges dominate the land. They affect the weather and the climate of vast areas.

There are mountains on all the continents. The highest ranges are in Asia. There are also mountains on the ocean floor, many of them rising above the seas as islands.

△ The setting sun lends a colorful glow to the peaks of Mt. Everest, the world's highest mountain. Trees grow on the lower slopes of high mountains, but the peaks are covered with ice and snow.

People live on mountains and in the valleys between them. The higher you go up a mountain, the thinner the air and the colder it gets.

The tops of high mountains are always covered in snow, even on a bright summer's day. Plants cannot grow above a certain level. Few animals, apart from insects and spiders, can live in the bitter cold of the snow-covered peaks.

△ A yak, a wild ox of Asia, grazes high up in the Himalaya mountains. Protected from the cold by its long, shaggy hair, the yak is well adapted to mountain conditions. Despite its size, it is an agile climber.

Looking at mountains

Mountain ranges of the world

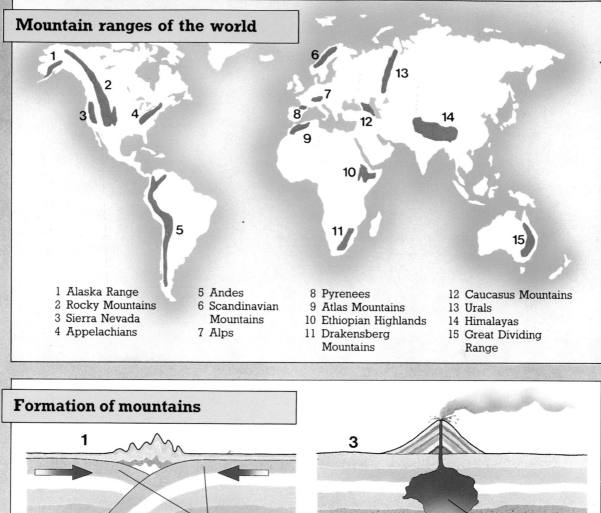

1 Alaska Range
2 Rocky Mountains
3 Sierra Nevada
4 Appelachians

5 Andes
6 Scandinavian
   Mountains
7 Alps

8 Pyrenees
9 Atlas Mountains
10 Ethiopian Highlands
11 Drakensberg
   Mountains

12 Caucasus Mountains
13 Urals
14 Himalayas
15 Great Dividing
   Range

Formation of mountains

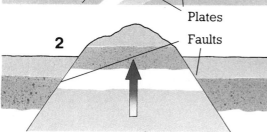

Mountains are formed in different ways, usually over long periods of time. Fold mountains (1) are pushed up by movements of large sections of the earth's crust called plates. Block mountains (2) form when cracks called faults develop in the crust. Volcanoes (3) appear when molten rock called magma erupts through the earth's surface. Dome mountains (4) form when the top layers of the earth are pushed up by rising magma.

How climate changes with height

The climate of a mountain changes with its height above sea level. A mountain near the equator has a range of climates, from polar at the top to tropical at the bottom.

Buzzard

①

5,000 m
(16,000 ft)

Hyrex

②

4,000 m
(13,000 ft)

Baboons

③

3,350 m
(11,000 ft)

Buffalos

④

3,000 m
(10,000 ft)

Leopard

Monkeys

⑤

1,650 m
(5,500 ft)

Elephant

Lion

Rhinoceros

⑥

1 Polar climate – permanent snow and ice
2 Alpine tundra – cold, bleak desert with little rainfall
3 Upland moor, like a temperate meadow
4 Upland grassland – tall grasses
5 Mountain rain forest – dense trees and heavy rains
6 Savanna – scattered trees on cultivated grassland

9

Kinds of mountains

Mountains are classified according to how they are formed. They are created in various ways by movements of plates in the earth's crust, mostly over a very long time.

Some mountains are formed by folding. Enormous pressures cause rock to fold up into mountains. Most of the world's great mountain ranges have been created in this way, including the Himalayas, the Rockies and the Alps.

△ The Alps are among the world's youngest fold mountains. They began to form about 25 million years ago.

Block, or fault block, mountains form when the earth's crust cracks. Great blocks move up or down along these cracks, or faults, in the earth's surface. Sometimes, a steep-walled valley is formed, with mountains on either side.

Molten rock from under the earth's crust also creates mountains. The molten rock, or magma, arches up the rocks above it to form dome mountains.

▽ The Sierra Nevada range in California is an example of block mountains, formed when a block of land was pushed up along faults in the earth's crust.

Volcanic mountains are created as magma reaches the earth's surface. They form in various shapes, depending on how explosive the eruption is and what materials are ejected.

Volcanoes are formed in groups or singly. There are volcanoes on land and on the seabed. Some volcanoes rise up from the sea above the water, forming islands.

△ The Cumbrian Mountains, in England's Lake District, are an example of dome mountains. They were pushed up by magma, which then cooled and hardened.

▷ Cotopaxi, in Ecuador, is one of the highest active volcanoes in the world. When it erupts, molten lava and hot ash pile up on its sides, building up its cone shape.

▽ A volcanic eruption on the ocean floor near Iceland, which began in 1963, built up the island of Surtsey.

The roof of the world

The Himalaya mountains, in Asia, are the world's highest. They occupy a vast area between northern India and Tibet. Much of the kingdom of Nepal lies in the Himalayas.

The region is often known as "The roof of the world." The chief range, the Great Himalayas, has an average height of 6,000 m (20,000 ft), with several peaks over 8,000 m (26,000 ft).

△ A monastery high in the Himalayas, where the highest peaks are permanently covered in snow.

▷ Mount Everest, the world's highest mountain, stands 8,848 m (29,029 ft) above sea level.

Other mountain ranges

Outside of Asia, the greatest mountain ranges are found in the western parts of the Americas. The Rocky Mountains, or Rockies, extend from the Yukon in northern Canada to New Mexico in the southern United States. The Andes run right down South America.

Mountains also provide spectacular scenery in all the other continents.

△ A glacier in the French Alps. These rivers of ice are found in cold mountain regions.

▷ The rugged Tetons, a range of the Rockies in northwestern Wyoming.

▽ The beautiful Lake Louise is set high in the Canadian Rockies, in southern Alberta.

△ The Cordillera Real, a range of the Andes mountains bordering Lake Titicaca, in South America.

◁ These strange but beautiful mountains rise above the banks of the Li river near Guilin, in southeast China.

▷ The Three Sisters, an outstanding feature of the Blue Mountains in Australia. The range forms part of the Great Dividing Range, along the eastern coast of the continent.

Life on mountains

Animals that live on mountains have become adapted to the rugged nature of the land. The wild goats and sheep of the mountains have soft pads on their hooves to help them climb up and down rocks and cliffs.

Smaller mammals either hibernate in winter or store up food. The craggy rocks provide good nesting places for many birds.

▽ An ibex in the French Alps. The ibex is a wild mountain goat found in the European Alps and the Himalayas.

Plant life on mountains varies with height and temperature. On the highest mountains there is a snowline above which nothing grows.

Below this is a cold zone where only mosses, lichens and the hardiest of grasses can grow. Lower down are zones of evergreen trees and then deciduous trees.

Flowers can flourish where trees cannot grow. They sprout high on mountainsides where the sun melts the snow in the summer months.

△ The snowline and the changing zones of vegetation can be clearly seen in this view of the Teton range in Wyoming.

21

People live in some of
the world's most
mountainous regions.

◁ People gather for a
Saturday market in a
village in Nepal, high up
in the Himalayas.

▷ A holiday resort in
the French Alps.

▽ The city of La Paz, in
Bolivia, lies on a plateau
in the Andes mountains.
At 3,630 m (11,909 ft)
above sea level, it is the
highest capital in the
world.

Mountains and the weather

High mountain ranges form huge barriers across the land and affect the weather and climate of the surrounding areas. Mountain weather itself varies with height.

The peaks of high mountains are covered in snow even in the tropics. They often poke up through the clouds. They can be wet and windy places. In winter, blizzards blow around the mountaintops.

△ Mountain peaks in the Himalayas poke through the clouds. The clouds form as moisture-laden air rises.

Coastal ranges are a good example of how mountains can affect the weather and climate of a region.

Winds that blow from the ocean rise and cool as they meet the mountains. As a result, they lose most of their moisture on the windward slopes in the form of rain or snow.

As the winds continue across the mountains, the dry air sinks down and warms the leeward slopes.

▽ Cone-bearing trees, which can withstand cold weather, grow on many mountain slopes. The upper limit of trees is called the tree line. Above it grow low shrubs, flowering plants and various grasses. Higher still are mosses and lichens.

Mountains under the sea

Mountains are not only found on land. Great ridges of mountains rise up from the ocean floor and in some places break the surface as islands. Iceland is such as island.

Many volcanoes rise from the seabed in the world's oceans. These, too, sometimes emerge as islands, like Hawaii and the West Indies.

△ White Island, a volcanic island off the northern coast of New Zealand.

Mountains and leisure

At mountain resorts, tourists enjoy the fresh mountain air, the scenic beauty and the winter skiing. Hiking, climbing and camping in the mountains are popular outdoor activities in the summer.

Mountains have always presented a great challenge to people who love adventure. Teams of climbers with oxygen and special equipment attempt the most difficult climbs. They brave terrible conditions to achieve their goal – to get to the top.

▽ With the help of ice axes and other equipment, a climber makes for the summit of Mt. Huntington, in Alaska.

The story of mountains

Mountain building

It is easy to see how mountains can be gradually worn away by erosion, the effect of wind and water or of glaciers. But is is not so easy to understand how they are formed, because this is a process that may take place over hundreds of millions of years.

△ A glacier inches down a mountain slowly wearing away the land.

Scientists have built up a picture of the inside of the earth by studying earthquakes. The earth has a rocky "skin" called the crust. This averages about 70 km (43 miles) in thickness. The crust and the top of the mantle (the layer under the crust) are made up of several huge sections called "plates." These plates move, or float, on a partly molten layer of rock inside the mantle. The movements are slow, not more than about 10 cm (4 inches) a year. But as the plates collide or move apart, they produce great force at the surface of the earth. These forces are responsible for the changes in the earth's crust – for the development of the continents as well as for the formation of mountains.

Folds and faults

Mountains form over millions of years at places where the earth's crust buckles and wrinkles and cracks. Great folds appear on the earth's surface in the form of mountain ranges. Large cracks, or faults, appear, and mountains are formed as huge blocks of rock move up and down. The fold and block mountains of today are examples of how this has happened in the past. These processes are still going on. New mountains are being created all the time, slowly over million of years.

The effect of molten rock

A much more dramatic form of

△ An artist's impression of the eruption of Mt. Mazama, in Oregon, nearly 7,000 years ago.

△ After the eruption, the top of the volcano collapsed. Today the deep hole is filled by Crater Lake.

mountain building occurs when molten rock under the earth's crust comes to the surface to form volcanoes.

Volcanoes build up over thousands of years. But a single violent eruption can have an immediate effect on the size of a mountain. An island might suddenly appear in the sea as an eruption of a volcano on the ocean floor shoots out material that builds up its top to break the surface. Or an explosion might blow the top off a mountain, drastically changing its height and shape.

Erosion

Another factor that changes the shape of mountains is erosion. This is caused by the weathering effect of wind and water or ice, which gradually wears away the rock. The eroded rock itself, from tiny particles to large fragments, is carried away by glaciers and rivers. As it moves, it scrapes against the land, carving out valleys. So even as new mountains are being formed and are rising upward, they are also being worn away by the effects of erosion.

△ The curious structures of Monument Valley, in Arizona, are the result of weathering by wind and water, which has worn away the surrounding rocks over thousands of years.

Facts and records

Highest and tallest

Mount Everest is the world's highest mountain above sea level. But it is not the tallest. Counting mountains on the ocean floor, the title of tallest peak belongs to Mauna Kea, in Hawaii. This active volcano stands 10.203 m (33,474 ft) above the seabed, in the Pacific Ocean. This is 1,355 m (4,445 ft) taller than Everest.

Avalanche!

One of the biggest hazards in mountain areas is the danger of an avalanche. This is a fall of a mass of material, including snow, ice, rocks or earth. It is often sudden, and can have devastating effects on people below. Whole villages have been covered by avalanches.

Avalanches usually happen when masses of snow or ice break off and fall down the mountainside, often taking earth and rocks with them. Local experts can usually tell from the weather conditions when avalanches are likely to occur. Warning notices are then posted or broadcast in the danger area.

△ The snow-capped peak of Mount Kilimanjaro.

△ An avalanche of snow comes roaring down a mountainside.

The snows of Kilimanjaro

Kilimanjaro, Africa's highest mountain, lies only a few degrees south of the equator, in northern Tanzania. Yet its peak is permanently covered in snow. Its climate changes from tropical at its base to polar at its peak, which stands 5,895 m (19,340 ft) above sea level.

Glossary

Block mountains
Mountains formed by earth movements along faults in the earth's crust; also called fault-block mountains.

Crust
The hard outer-shell of the earth.

Deciduous trees
Trees that lose their leaves for part of every year.

Dome mountains
Mountains formed by the force of magma pushing upward but solidifying below the surface of the earth.

Erosion
The wearing away of rocks and other parts of the land. It is caused by running water, wind, ice and snow.

Eruption
A volcanic eruption occurs when molten rock, gases and steam are forced to the surface from inside the earth through a volcano. Lava and hot ash from volcanoes pile up to form mountains.

Fault
A crack in the earth's crust along which rocks have moved.

Fold mountains
Mountains pushed up by earth movements into a fold or ridge. Most of the world's great mountain ranges are fold mountains.

Glacier
A mass of ice that moves very slowly down a valley under the force of gravity, gradually deepening and widening the valley. This process of wearing away the land is called glaciation.

Lava
Molten rock flowing out of a volcano.

Magma
Molten rock below the earth's surface.

Plates
Great sections of the earth's hard outer layers that float very slowly on a partly molten layer of rock.

Volcanoes
Openings on the earth's surface through which material from inside the earth is forced out. Mountains made of the material are also called volcanoes.

Index